Words Once Hidden

By Praise T. Nwanegbo

Copyright 2021

Foreword

I have read many poetry books but this one is my favorite. The emotions and feelings touched by the writer are those that are so far away yet so near, basic and relatable. But she boldly and delicately touches every note of their sound in a subtle but true way giving us a chance to touch the pure flesh of our own emotions with words that are also music. I have never read poems like these anywhere else. These poems give feelings a face and emotions a body that can only be so vivid yet so blurry. With these poems you can touch the emotions that have always escaped you, you can see their different faces.

I enjoyed each poem with so much thrill.

...Dumbfounded reader.

Table of Contents

Is This Your Philosophy?

Lend me your ears

so I can preach the gospel of salvation from the depths of my heart

Lend me your ears

so I can whisper heavy words of reason

Lend me your ears

so I can tell you the story of our ancestors

the time of great wisdom and truth

where all wasn't lost

Lend me your heart

so that I can mend the fragmented pieces

Lend me those eyes

so that I can show you my world

that I have so desperately built and broken down

Show me the eyes you used

to water the plant of redemption

Bring forth those hands

that carried the pain of others

until they were blistered and bruised

Is Humanity nothing but a fairytale?

A story told to the naïve

For those innocent enough to believe it's true

those hopelessly in need for something to cling on to?

The desperate and the passionate

Those whose cynicism hasn't blinded

their path to atonement?

The Lady In Blue

Her silk dress waltzing to the screams of the wind

Eyes hollow and empty

as her tears swallow the ground beneath her

Her silent cries piercing the ears of the sky

Her tongue stolen from her

Yet she sings a captivating song

Ending it with an eerie laugh

Her raven-coloured hair did nothing

but elegantly rest on her shoulders

with wild curls that looked mad yet majestic

Her skin was as dark as day

and her heart shone like void stars

She was the epitome of chaos and disorder

mess and turmoil

disarray and everything good

Art Of Me

I have mastered the art of hiding myself

The art of being what others think of me

Being ready to constantly please others despite my discomfort

'Thank you', 'I am sorry'

continuously flowing from my lips

like a leaking sink that can't be fixed

in fear of offending somebody

Almost religiously ignoring my satisfaction

After a long day

of doing what's expected of me

I lock myself up

in the safety of my room

My four walls

My haven

Where my thoughts run wild

but never get too close to hurt me

But yet

the only thing I worry about

is the next day

The day I start it all over again

neglecting me

Behold, this is the art of me

Beauty And Beyond

Am I beautiful?

Does the sun cast its warm glow onto the earth?

Am I beautiful?

Does the sky rage with stars and embrace the moon at night?

Do trees stand tall and marigolds grow towards the heavens?

Does the wind howl with songs and kisses those it passes by?

Is there air to breathe even though gone souls may grieve?

Do the waters dance gracefully across creation?

Am I beautiful?

As long as the sun comes in the morning to grace us

with its warmth and kind glow

and the moon travels to us at night

to caress the night sky

and peck the darkness with its stars

You are beautiful

as long as the heavens remain

Against All Odds

It was dark in my tiny bubble
I wasn't smart enough
Not pretty enough
Not good enough

Every day seemed to get harder than the last
I pushed through
because I thought it would get better
or at least I hoped

Soon I was getting dragged
lower and lower
into the pit of salty self-pity

Then anxiety kicked in
and in strolled insecurity
with its head high and a smirk
with an agenda to ruin everything before it

The constant fear of never being good enough
held me by the throat
Fear of rejection
smothered me
that I thought my mere presence
was irritating

Then a light emerged
Blinding me briefly
somewhere within that light was hope

I couldn't see it but I could feel it consuming my whole being

It was strange but it was wholesome
It was kind and filled me with warmth
It was safe and liberating
It was fire that illuminated my soul
and ignited a new treasured feeling within

3 Am

What do I do when my heart swells up painfully

Rapidly filling up with uncharted emotions

What do I say to myself

when I'm drowning in my own words

My head clouded

the sky's got nothing on me

No wave is stronger

than the thoughts rushing through my mind

I can barely lie still

The drunk yells of my heart are unbearable

It's 3 am

I'm tired

but I'm nowhere close

to feeling the heaviness

of my eyelids

The heaviness dwells in my soul

at this hour

It's 3:01

Rejection

Another way of saying

you are not good enough

Another way of saying

you are not worthy

Are they right?

I mean they must be

if you are there standing and gawking

at your unfortunate and miserable situation

Right?

Are you going to let it live with you?

Tear you from inside out

destroy your confidence

and the walls of your self-esteem

or are you going to turn around

and use that rejection as reason

A reason to move forward

to succeed

to let go

Rejection is lethal

But it cannot break you

if you do not let it

It wants you

to face a calamitous defeat

Though no matter how unwanted you may feel

How it makes your head heavy with confusion

No matter how it may seem

like it is snapping your bones

and tearing your skin

Do not let it consume you, crush you,

squash you beneath its wicked boots

as if you were nothing

but a bug in the dirt

I had to move from my position

before I got trampled

I had to find a position higher

than those that tossed me aside

Making them unable to wreck me

They said I couldn't, so I will

Run, They Said

Run wild

she said

No one likes a quiet one

Run like the wind

he said

You need to be fast

to escape the condemnation of reality

The muddy rum coloured streets

sit beneath my muddy cold riddled feet

Step after step the pain pierced

not just my feet

It pierced not just my mind

It pierced deep within the core of my being

It pierced more than my soul

But run they said,

failing to see my agony

or simply ignoring my suffering

Run they said

fools

forgetting that this pain

is a fabrication of the mind

and mine is running wild

The Chronicles Of Self-destruction

First came the smiles

There were a lot

All were fake

never genuine

But then came the tears

They flowed like a river

They came so fiercely

They never stopped

Tears galore

Hot and painful

they kept rushing

The tears were immune

to the insincerity of my smile

How deceitful and dishonest it was

The tears never lifted, never dried

After that was the anger

immense anger

that held me bound

What say I break free?

From this road that may only lead

to the destruction of my mind

Thus Is Fear

Fear

what a lethal thing

what a nonsensical thing

What a time-wasting thing

Fear

such a hateful thing

Such a painful thing

Such a dangerous thing

Because of fear

many have destroyed their opportunities

and have justified

their recklessness and failures

with fear

They have adjusted their morals

to accommodate fear

To speak up for fear

Fear is immature and uneducated

but even the wise and the scholars

fall for its tricks

Fear is when your soul

trembles with surfeit uncertainty

Fear is where hopes and dreams perish

Fear is insecurity

Fear is extinction

The fear of finding
The fear of losing
The fear of hurting
The fear of loving
The fear of not being loved

Fear is human

Sound Of Sunlight

Wiggling my toes
Is all I can do
My mind is nothing but fuzzy
None of my thoughts stick

Floating from place to place
I cannot seem to hold on to them
My mind is lost in the abyss
like it's on a voyage of deliverance
that will never be found

My mind feels lost
like it isn't mine
Foreign and uncomfortable
Like it doesn't fit

My heart feels strange
like it isn't there
Empty and quiet
like it's hiding

I'm so sick
of the constant murmuring
that I can't seem to grasp

The darkness is so vivid
it's overwhelming and blinding
But sadly
it has been years

I have grown accustomed to the dull ache in my chest

and the tired breaths I let

What state is this?

Sea Of Emotion

It's like I'm feeling everything yet nothing at once

It's consuming

It's further than the ends of the abyss

But closer than the blood

that courses through my veins

It feels so foreign to me

but somehow I can call it by its name

One can get lost in this sea

It is like a tornado trying to rip me apart

But also like the serenity of a mother cuddling her sleeping child

These emotions are cunning

They play tricks on the mind

Allowing me to believe

that without it

I'm not me

Questions Of Contentment

I am content
I am in a state of contentment
Is it blissful?
I'm not sure

But am I happy?
I'm not sure
Should I strive for the absolute goal of happiness?
But am I ready for the hardship
that comes with pursuing this goal?
Am I strong enough?
Am I worthy of this goal?
Do I deserve it?

To be happy do we have to struggle first?
I don't think I am ready yet

I am somewhat comfortable in the half-hearted seat of contentment
I'm not sad
Isn't that enough?

My heart doesn't flutter
from the warmth of this so called happiness
it's probably just a myth

Those claiming to be happy
are nothing more but content creatures
temporary out of their zone of struggle
But look, I am distracted from the things that use to cause me pain
Truly that has to be enough

I guess that'll have to do for now
At least until I get strong enough

At least until am ready to care enough
At least until I want it enough
that I will not think of the hard journey
but keep my eyes focused on my goal
On the state of happiness
However, I'm content
in this state of contentment

Still I Smile

Some people smile through the hard times

when their life seems to be falling apart around them

Some look up to the sky

at the break of dawn,

the time where the sky is tinted with a soft pink hue

embraced with a tiny portion of orange

married together peacefully

on the blue of the night sky

that is packing its bag

getting ready to leave

so that the bright blue canvas can soon take its shift,

but the moon is still there

quietly fading into oblivion

waiting to darken another world

How can a world so beautiful

want to hurt me

or cause me pain

The sky taught me the most important lesson

a simple but essential lesson

'Don't give up, it will get better'

Even at that moment, that very moment

where I thought giving up

was the only solution left

Just like in the dark of the night sky

the moon will shine through

Redemption At Sunset

He gave his only begotten son to die for our sins
To die for us who had forsaken him
For us who are not worthy of his thoughts
He laid down his life for us
He bled and he cried

Taking the punishment that we fully deserved
With blood flowing from his eyes
Rusty nails becoming one with his palms

His screams of agony
So that we could be saved
Yet we dare turn our backs on him

Our negligence has pushed us into the well of sin
Our hands are tainted with transgression
yet we touch his garment with hopes for salvation
but yet he welcomes us with open arms

And we were strangers watching
So disconnected from the one who gave us life
Consumed with regret and reflection
With an attempted defeat by temptation

On the brink of losing hope
I'm tired, fighting in a losing battle
I'm weak, burdened with reality
I'm desperate

I'll put aside my pride
Put away my ego
have mercy

The war in my heart rages
I can't make it on my own
I've reached the point of giving up

almost sacrificing myself to the dogs

Then, I heard a call
a whisper
my heart drawn to it
It said my name
with overwhelming love

I felt safe, the war in my chest settling

Some May Not Understand

I misbehave

to hide what lies behind the curtain

I retaliate

to prove that I should not be messed with

I step up

because I will not hide from monsters

I speak up

because I experienced the hurt

I stand tall

to tell you I will not be moved

I fight back because

I owe myself at least that

The pain is mine and mine alone

I do as I wish

I will take the pain

and bury it deep within

Some say it's unhealthy

that I should confront my pain, make peace with it first

Peace?

What courtesy has peace shown me

that it deserves to be brought into the equation?

It sits there on it horse

Thinking once we say we have made peace with pain

it will gallop into a field of roses and life will bloom

But life itself is easier written than lived

Does peace exist anywhere on this earth

I have made my peace with life is what you want to hear?

I have faith in a better tomorrow

Does that satisfy your ears?

But maybe that's just my cynicism talking

lurking behind the curtains of my mind

Home Is A Home

Aggressively drowning out my thoughts
Holding my tears at gunpoint
daring them to fall
Squeezing my eyes tightly shut
praying that my thoughts would just suffocate themselves

But it stands there
stronger than ever
with its feet buried into the ground
taking a stance of resistance

My cries linger in the air
Tiny whimpers fall from my lips
Blood draws from my tongue
as I force my cries silent

The pain evading my senses
Nothing makes sense at that point
except for the pain
banging on the doors of my mind
rattling the cage of my mind

The fortress that I strove
to protect at all cost
all breaking down
and withering away around me
Disintegrating into mocking bits
that I cannot hold onto

I can hear the laughs
of what I strove to build
They're laughing
laughing at my failure
Attempting to stay sane

as the world I had built with tears
slowly but rapidly
crashes at my feet
my home is gone

But I will build another

Her Majesty

We have redefined

the lines that were set by our ancestors

The world now rages with thunder

brought down by the evil of our tongues

screaming to be let out of the bondage

that we so wickedly trapped her in

Rocking the cages of her confinement

Nothing makes more sense

than the soothing shrills that dance from her lips

Her cries are our norm

for we are so used to the darkness

that has been cast

upon our earth

upon her

Cleaning up our disgorge from her eyes

so she can see what she has truly become

A pile of sickening bones

left by the dogs on the earth

the ones who kill and

effortlessly destroy

Heaves of loneliness poison her

she has never felt so disgusted

She dreams of the times

when she was once draped

in the finest silk

Drenched in jewels

found from deep within her

She was crowned with the desires of her dwellers

and nothing could defeat her purpose

Oh her majesty

how we have so wickedly tarnished your grace

Genesis Of Her Conviction

Could it be our hearts waiting to self-destruct

Could it be our souls waiting to feel the rust of time

Our names engraved into the stones

as we are buried six feet under

consumed with regret and reflection

Might I wait for the moment my heart ceased to beat

or wait for my lungs to darken and turn to ash

Should I cry on mountains

expecting it to be moved by my tears

Could I hold my head high

and run through the wilderness

Should I open my mouth wide

and allow a loud yet melodic symphony to flow

May I step on the cruel words thrown at my heart

Or should I sit there

and wait for those very words

to tear me apart.

Screaming at dusk

blaming it for my failure

Should I stand around

hoping that something would happen?

Is this me avoiding risks?

Maybe it's my stubbornness

that's drawing me back

Drawing me back from living my life

From growing old with no painful regret

From doing the things that my heart wishes

And from being me

Simply me

Malignant Tongue

You make it sound so vain

A slip of a tongue

and all of a sudden

you're spiraling down into the pit of shame

You make it sound so pathetic

Close your eyes

for just a second

next thing you know

the eyes of judgement are cast upon you

like a creature descending its ugly breath on you

You have no idea

the power your tongue holds

The words you utter

cannot even be carried by ten giants

yet you laugh so easily with

no care in the world

Yet you speak with such ease

that even the ones you cast down

with your vicious tongue

turn to look at you with reverence

Misplaced adoration

Their will has been soaked in bleach

scrubbed of all sense and reasoning

Even I the one that spits on you

with tremendous disgust

can't help but see

Memories Of Bygones

In that very minute
In the midst of it all
It could feel so painful
like you couldn't possibly move on
from that very situation
Like that very event itself
is life-altering

The harsh and painful sore on your heart, agonizing
That very minute, overwhelming
But as time passes,
No matter how slow time might seem to crawl
That very minute becomes a faint scar
When you think about it
it's distant but still somewhat vivid
You can feel its presence radiating
like it is so close, so close you can touch it
with just one small breath
the feeling of that very minute
is forcing itself to remain relevant
whilst your mind and your heart is explaining why it isn't

It's like a child
constantly and aggravatingly attempting
to get your attention

The past
something we can't change no matter how much we try
The scar of the past
so present but yet couldn't be further

Whether we like it or not
No matter how much we know

We can't change the past
we must accept it
We accept that, yes we experienced the hurt
But we can move on

We will move on
The past is nothing but memories
Though they are ones we can learn from
nevertheless they remain
unchangeable bygones

One Shade Of Change

Met with the warm smile of dusk

Its fading dye

the faint whispers of orange

growing quieter

Maybe nothing lasts forever

Even the things we were so sure would

You were convinced

with all your being

that it will last

but no, it too passed

But then maybe it was a good thing

that it didn't last

Maybe it happened

so that you could move on

to something better

A new dawn soon approaching

Albeit, things are constantly changing

It's understandable

that in that moment of change

Everything seems unstable

like the world itself is shaking

trying to find its balance again

Even if it's for a second or a day

the world had been flipped on its head

turned completely upside-down

That very moment

can feel utterly terrifying

That one shade of change

Simply preparing you

for the other shades to come

Cracked

The confidence I must find in myself
That confidence
that seems like it might simply be a myth
One only spoken about
in an attempt at reconsidering
your philosophy on yourself

One that might be forgotten
Or perhaps covered
in dirt and low self-esteem
Self-loathing and self-pity
A false idea of what I thought I should be

I look at others
and I can't help but compare
myself to what I lack
How I don't look as pretty
How my clothes
just don't fit right
How my hair
doesn't cascade down my back

My lack of beauty
My lack of intelligence
My lack of skill
So consumed with weakness
and my assumed shortcomings
Going crazy
trying to grasp at perfection

What a pity
Exhausted with the constant need to compare

that the switch went off
Just like that, I didn't care

Perhaps I couldn't care
I didn't care that they were prettier
than me
or smarter than me
I didn't care that their hair
looked only the way I wish mine could
I was so tired of it
that I simply had no choice
than to accept myself
the way I was
and move on

What Is Happiness?

I must find my happiness
from myself
And for myself

For my happiness to start
and end with another
that very thought
frightens me

I can't depend
on another person
for my happiness
I want to be a person
who's found their happiness
in themselves first
For my happiness to be dependent on another
that I do not want
That is what I despise

But then again
What is happiness?
And is it mine alone
or is it one that must be shared?

Is happiness
where your heart and mind are at peace?
No sadness clouding over your soul
No darkness intruding into your thoughts
Pure bliss?

Is happiness
something you have to fight tooth and nail for?
Or is it something
that just falls onto your lap

Maybe happiness is love
Love for yourself

Perhaps happiness is all in our mind
Our mindset
Maybe

How we think
and approach the world
How we see others
and feel towards it
Our perspective

Maybe happiness can be found on a spectrum
between peace and misery
But that's simply speculation
Perhaps happiness was never meant to be understood

Perhaps there is no true meaning of happiness
Perhaps you'll just know when you're happy

What does happiness feel like?
I can't seem to grasp onto it or comprehend it

What is happiness?

Curiosity

Is it possible

to be curious about everything

yet nothing at all?

Curious enough

to to do the bare minimum

but not enough to delve deep

and fully quench that curiosity

Just curious enough

to satisfy that initial interest

Where you know enough to say:

'Yes, I have heard about it'

Maybe spit out a few facts

But not to the point

where you can give your in-depth thoughts

So when I'm asked

'What am I interested in?'

I can't help but think

'Nothing, nothing at all'

Moments In Time

It seems so funny

How I can look back into my hazy memories

and laugh or even flinch

How I can stare right into the blur of the moments

that have disappeared

And cry or feel that dull ache

of the sadness that is withering away

But I can never seem to truly block out those emotions

Because they never really disappear

do they?

Never truly perish

They feel like they are hidden

deep within me

Though a faint memory

they feel vividly distant

Time does nothing but push it back

into the depths of mind

I have to accept

that past situations have passed

It's so surreal

But the emotions left are beyond real

At that very moment

it felt like it could have lasted forever

But now

it is nothing but a dull throbbing

That moment

could have felt like the worst

or best time in my life

But at the end of the day

no matter how wonderful or miserable that moment was

it passed

Trapped in a place

that I can no longer allow

to interfere with my present

And here

I am somewhere in time

Here

I am looking back at how it all was

And how

it all has passed

How the past

remained in the past

Harsh Sky

The world feels
like it's about to crash at my feet'
Such an old song

But the sky seems so relaxed
Untouched and unfazed by my troubles
Like everything isn't hanging by its hinges
As if
with one little breath
everything won't crush down
with a heart-shattering bang

The sky seems
like it doesn't care
that the walls closing in around me
are grey

The sky seems harsh to me
even with its gentle smile
that seems so patronizing
and that calm gaze
that holds something else I can't understand
Like it's mocking me so passively

I try to focus on the sky
as the ground shakes so furiously
But the sky mocks me

I know it does

How can it look so calm and tranquil

while it's looking at such ruin and distress

Does the blue sky not care?

Its cotton veil sits so relaxedly in its place

Even the starry sky doesn't seem bothered

It looks so consumed with tranquillity

It's stars somewhat blinding

Why is it so peaceful

when around me I know a war might break out?

Why is the sky so calm

when everything else is in anguish?

Share with me your secret

Broken Alliance

Dangerous

I am broken

Beautiful

I shine

Useful

but I am fragile

I cannot continue to live like this

Though we have had our times and laughs

Our journey

is sadly coming to its end

I hoped this would never happen

However, I was ignorant

to the humour of this world

And the storm changed our course

It threw us in different directions

Now we must bid farewell

Sadness I feel

but relief dwells within me as well

For the reason that I can start a fresh passage through life

My own odyssey

Guilty I feel

but I am ready

to wash my hands clean of this and move on

I cannot stop my journey

the turbulence has separated our paths

and all that is left

is to continue from where we are

broken

I thought our bond was strong

an unbreakable alliance

But I suppose at the end of the day

it was all made of glass

As I continue my journey

I must continue to find

and understand myself

There is more ahead of me

the moment I am in

is not all that there is

But I must say

at the end of the day

Dangerous

I am broken

Beautiful

I shine

But I too

am made of glass

To Care, Or My Sanity?

The truth is that I do care

I have mastered the art of not caring

that all it did

was mask the fact that I care too much

I told myself

that I had to stop caring

for the sake of my sanity

My mother always told me

I take things too far

I got to a point

where I believed

that caring

was not even an option anymore

That it will be

the destruction of what I had left of myself

I looked at things that would have hurt me in the past

but could not help but roll my eyes

at the pitiful humour of it all

I did not care that I was sad

I convinced myself

that it's only for the best

I did not care

that I was lonely

I convinced myself
that with people around me
I can't possibly be lonely
I just did not care
I convinced myself
that not caring will pay off
in the end

Even then
I was still scared
that this empty feeling inside
This feeling of not caring
would be too much
one day

But I cared
too much that I couldn't differentiate
that act of caring and the act of not
Maybe it was because my heart
did not pound when I was nervous anymore
Or skip when I was happy
Just there
supposedly void of emotions and movement

But there are days
when the feelings come rushing in
Those are the days I know care

Those are the days that my emotions

are beyond overwhelming

The days that one little look

can cause me to spiral and crush down

One little word can shatter my self-security

One tiny action destroying the armour I built

But strangely enough

those days

the days that feel like it can swallow me whole

are the days I feel the most human

Bridge

You on the other side

What colour is the morning sky?

Is it grim and murky

like it is here?

How is the breeze

that kisses your skin?

It is nothing but a storm here

When do the flowers bloom?

Here flowers don't exist anymore

You on the other side

Can I come

and rest where you are?

But I am afraid

of the stain I might leave in my wake

What if the blue sky turns cloudy and dim?

And the breeze starts to breathe harshly

What if the flowers start to wither and turn to ash

Perhaps we should destroy the bridge

Then this way it will remain beautiful on your side

At least I can keep a picture of the splendour

I can imagine the friendly sun on my skin

The earth's breath walking beside me

I can imagine the flowers growing towards the heavens

The colour of each petal radiating

53

You on the other side

Let us destroy this bridge

Let us keep our differences

Nothing good can come of it anyway